Fact Finders®

Amusement Park Science

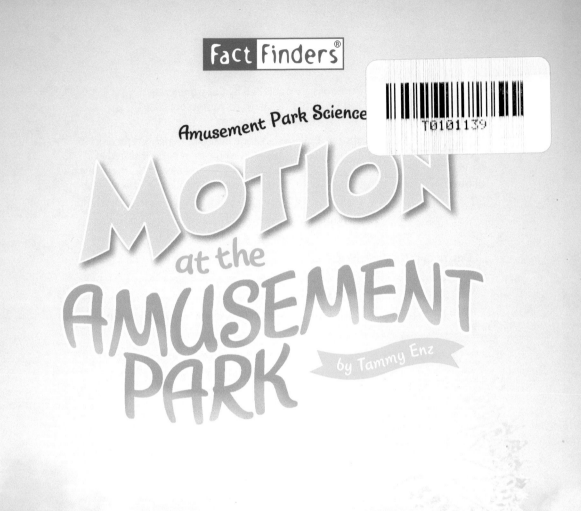

MOTION
at the
AMUSEMENT PARK

by Tammy Enz

CAPSTONE PRESS
a capstone imprint

Fact Finders Books are published by Capstone Press,
1710 Roe Crest Drive, North Mankato, Minnesota 56003
www.capstonepub.com

Library of Congress Cataloging-in-Publication Data
Names: Enz, Tammy, author.

Title: Motion at the amusement park / by Tammy Enz.

Description: North Mankato, Minnesota : an imprint of Capstone Press, [2020]
| Series: Fact finders. Amusement park science | Audience: Ages 8-11. |
Audience: Grades 4 to 6.

Identifiers: LCCN 2018060534| ISBN 9781543572858 (hardcover) | ISBN
9781543575248 (pbk.) | ISBN 9781543572896 (ebook pdf)

Subjects: LCSH: Motion—Juvenile literature. | Force and energy--Juvenile
literature. | Amusement parks—Juvenile literature.

Classification: LCC QC133.5 .E59 2020 | DDC 531/.11—dc23

LC record available at https://lccn.loc.gov/2018060534

Editorial Credits
Carrie Braulick Sheely, editor; Tracy McCabe, designer; Eric Gohl, media researcher;
Kathy McColley, production specialist

Photo Credits
Alamy: Skip Caplan, 12; iStockphoto: briannolan, 23, CasarsaGuru, 19, 25,
Photomick, 27, tacojim, 13; Newscom/ZUMA Press: Kyle Grantham, 11,
Sam Gangwer, 9; Shutterstock: ChameleonsEye, back cover (background), 1
(background), 15, Chris Howey, 17, Doug Lemke, 7, George Sheldon, 29, I Wei
Huang, 16, Krylovochka, cover (bottom), 1 (bottom), Maria Bell, 5, Shooting Star
Studio, 21; SuperStock: agf photo, cover (top)

Design Elements: Shutterstock

TABLE of CONTENTS

CHAPTER 1

MOTION RULES!

Spinning. Looping. Swinging. Dropping. Wherever you look in the amusement park, you'll see motion. Motion is the key to nonstop thrills and stomach-dropping fun. It keeps you looping on the roller coaster, spinning on the Tilt-a-Whirl, and crashing in the bumper cars.

Motion simply means movement. All the head-spinning, eye-popping motion at an amusement park might seem random and out of control. But motion follows the laws of physics.

Want to see how the laws of motion work? Strap yourself in for a wild ride, and let's get moving!

physics—the study of matter and energy, including light, heat, electricity, and motion

As the drop tower ride speeds downward, it can reach 60 miles (97 km) per hour.

FACT:
In 2017, the top 25 amusement parks in the world had 244 million visitors.

The Laws of Motion

All motion follows the same rules. Famous scientist Sir Isaac Newton studied and defined the rules of motion more than 300 years ago. Newton's three laws are:

1. Objects that are moving keep moving without changing direction. Objects that aren't moving stay still. A force must act on an object to change its motion. A force is a pushing or pulling action. Newton's first law is also called the law of inertia.

2. The change in an object's motion depends on its mass and the strength of force applied to it. The mass of an object is all the stuff that makes up the object. This law says that the more mass an object has, the greater the force needed to accelerate it. To accelerate something means to get it moving or speed it up.

3. For every action there is an equal and opposite reaction. This means for every force or movement, there is an equal force or movement that reacts.

accelerate—to change the speed of a moving object

inertia—the tendency of an object to stay at rest or in an existing state of motion in a straight line unless acted on by a force

mass—the matter an object contains

Roller coasters follow Newton's laws of motion as they speed around the track.

THE LEGEND OF SIR ISAAC NEWTON

Isaac Newton isn't just known for describing the laws of motion. He is also known for discovering gravity. People tell a famous legend about how he made this discovery. The story says that as Newton sat by a tree, he watched an apple fall. Most people wouldn't give this event a second thought. But the falling apple made Newton question what was pulling it straight down instead of in a different direction. His curiosity led to his discovery of the force of gravity.

gravity—a force that pulls objects with mass together; gravity pulls objects down toward the center of Earth

CHAPTER 2

INERTIA AT WORK

How does inertia work? You've seen it if you've dropped a ball on a smooth surface. It just keeps rolling. Its motion will change if you grab the ball or it hits something and stops. If left alone, it will eventually slow down and stop. That is because a force called friction acted upon the ball as it rolled.

You can find inertia all around at the amusement park. Look no further than a roller coaster! Did you know that an engine doesn't power a roller coaster? A cable system with gears pulls it up that first big hill. From there other forces are at work. The force of gravity pulls it down. Inertia keeps it rolling through more hills and loops. And as it moves, friction between the cars and the track helps it slow down. Eventually, braking force brings the thrilling ride to a full stop.

friction—the force caused by objects rubbing together

You see inertia at work on the Tilt-a-Whirl too. Once your seat gets spinning, it just keeps spinning. Another force can act on the ride to speed up or slow down your spinning. This can happen when the ride changes speed or as you go up and down on the sloped platform. You might even begin spinning in the opposite direction. But to change your spinning motion, there needs to be enough force to resist inertia.

The Tilt-a-Whirl moves along a track as it spins.

Inertia and the Rotor Ride

Hop on the rotor ride for another look at inertia. You stand inside a cylindrical room. The room begins spinning. You're spinning around and around. Then, surprise! The floor drops out! But you stay stuck to the wall. Why?

Think about this. Have you ever tied an object to a string and spun it over your head? What happens when you let go? The object keeps moving straight out in the direction it was headed when you let go. That's inertia at work. The string provides a force called centripetal force to keep the object traveling in a circle until you let go.

You are like that object in the rotor ride. This time, it's the walls that keep you from flying off in a straight line. While inertia tries to push you outward the walls force you inward. In fact, their force is so strong that you don't even need the floor to hold you up. When it drops away, you still cling to the wall.

When the bottom drops out, riders stay forced against the wall on the rotor ride.

centripetal force—a force that pulls spinning objects to the center of a circle

cylindrical—having a shape with flat, circular ends and sides shaped like a tube

Inertia at Rest

Inertia also keeps things at rest. You can stare all day at that pyramid of bottles at the bottle toss game. But inertia will keep those bottles where they are. They'll only move when you hit them with the softball you toss at them. *Smash!* The thrown ball applies the force needed to get the bottles moving—and hopefully win you a prize!

Inertia would also let you sit all day at the top of the Ferris wheel if forces didn't act on the ride. Forces come from motors, gravity, and other sources. These forces pull and push on the Ferris wheel and many other rides to get them going.

Without forces, you could sit at the top of a Ferris wheel all day.

Changing Direction

Now you've learned two parts of Newton's first law. Objects need forces to get them moving. They also need forces to stop their motion. But there is a third part to Newton's first law. It states that objects need forces to change direction.

Imagine yourself at the very top of a pendulum ride. If you were to drop an object from up there, the force of gravity would pull it straight down to the ground. But when the ride swings downward, you don't fall straight down. You swing around in a semicircle. Why? It's because the arm attached to your seat changes your direction. It applies centripetal force to keep you traveling in a circular motion.

Inertia would send you flying straight off the roller coaster. But the cars are connected to the track. The design of the track forces you to change direction. It sends you through curves and loops. It doesn't allow your car to go sailing in the direction inertia would send it. It changes your direction.

centripetal force—a force that pulls spinning objects to the center of a circle

pendulum—a weight that hangs from a fixed point and swings back and forth freely using the force of gravity

Forces don't need to be directly in contact with something to make them change their direction. When you toss a ball into the air, gravity pulls it down. Gravity acts on the dart you toss in the balloon game too. You need to toss it a bit higher than your target. Why? Gravity begins pulling the dart down as it moves forward.

Centripetal force acts on the pendulum ride to keep it going in a semicircle.

CHAPTER 3

THE FORCE OF MOTION

You look in the distance and see a musician carrying a tuba. You also see people carrying big stuffed animals. Which do you think takes more effort to move? The tuba takes more effort, or force, to get moving. Newton's second law explains why. This law says that the more mass an object has, the greater the force needed to get it moving, or accelerating. The tuba has more mass than the stuffed animal.

A massive Ferris wheel needs a great deal of force to get it going.

You'll see this law at work on the rides too. The more massive the ride, the greater the force needed to get it going and to stop it. It doesn't take much force to get yourself swinging high on a swing set because you have a small mass. But a massive Ferris wheel needs the force of big motors to get it going.

FACT:
George Washington Gale Ferris Jr. built the first Ferris wheel for the World's Fair in 1893. This huge machine weighed 1,300 tons. Riders could see 25 miles (40 km) from its 25-story height.

F=MA

A simple equation describes Newton's second law: F=ma.

The *F* in the formula stands for force.

The *m* stands for mass.

The *a* stands for acceleration.

The law states that you need a bigger force to get a bigger mass moving. But it works the other way too. Moving objects with more mass will create a more forceful impact.

This formula explains why you feel a greater impact when getting slammed into by a big guy in the bumper cars than getting bumped by a little kid. You might also see this rule at work at the dive show. A diver with more mass will hit the water with more force—and usually make a bigger splash!

Force, mass, and acceleration work together. A change in one will mean that another will also need to change.

---

impact—a forceful contact of objects

The riders on the left can create a more forceful impact than the rider on the right because they have more mass.

SPEED, VELOCITY, AND ACCELERATION

When people talk about motion, they might mention an object's speed, velocity, or acceleration. They aren't the same. But they are closely related. Speed tells how fast something is moving. Velocity is similar to speed, but it also tells the direction something is traveling. Acceleration is different. Acceleration is how fast something is speeding up or slowing down. When a car starts from a stop, it's accelerating. Its speed is always changing. Once it gets up to a constant speed, its acceleration is zero.

FACT:
The fastest roller coaster in the world is the Formula Rossa in the United Arab Emirates. It has a top speed of 149.1 miles (239 km) per hour.

Impact!

Which packs a bigger punch? Getting plowed into by someone coming full speed off the bottom of the waterslide? Or is the force bigger if you get bumped into by a bumper boat on the lazy river? You guessed it. The speedy slider will cause the biggest impact because his acceleration is greater. The F=ma formula shows that larger accelerations cause bigger forces.

You'll see how acceleration affects force when you play the carnival games too. What happens when you toss a ball at a stack of bottles? You wind up and throw with all your strength, right? Why? You want to hit the bottles with as much force as you can. The faster you can get the ball going, the more likely you'll knock over the bottles. You need a big force to pack the punch that wins the prize!

Riders speeding down a waterslide can create a forceful impact.

FACT:

Did you know that gravity is an acceleration? As objects fall, they speed up. For falling objects the a in the F=ma equation can be replaced with g. The g stands for the acceleration of gravity.

Momentum

When would it be easier to stop a roller coaster? Would it be when it is halfway down that first death-defying drop? Or would it be easier near the end of the track as it gently rolls down the straight part? That's right. It would take more force to stop the ride at its maximum acceleration. This is because of momentum. Momentum depends on an object's mass and velocity. Velocity is a measurement of the speed and direction an object is moving.

Newton's second law explains how momentum works. When an object is accelerating it has momentum. It takes more force to stop something with more acceleration. The faster something is accelerating, the more momentum it gains.

Momentum is at play in many amusement park rides. You'll see it in pendulum rides. Momentum is what swings you back up after you swing downward. Momentum is key in the back and forth swinging of a pendulum. It allows you to keep swinging.

momentum—the amount of force in a moving object determined by the object's mass and velocity

A roller coaster has a great deal of momentum as it speeds down the first hill.

CHAPTER 4

EQUAL AND OPPOSITE

Now it's time to look for Newton's third law of motion at the park. This law states that for every action there is an equal and opposite reaction. An action is a force that an object exerts on something. A reaction is the force that pushes back.

When you ram into another bumper car, you'll notice that both cars bounce back from each other. The action happens when the cars hit. The reaction is when they bounce away. They bounce away from each other with the same amount of force and in opposite directions than they were traveling when they hit. Magnitude describes how big the movement of the cars is.

The lazy river gives us another example of Newton's third law. You get your tube to move forward by paddling backward. The action is you pushing the water back. The reaction is your tube moving forward. The more you push, the more you move forward.

After two bumper cars hit, they bounce back in the opposite direction.

THE ENERGY OF IMPACT

Impacts cause more than motion. They also release energy. How do we know? We can hear it and feel it. The crashing noise you hear when two cars hit is energy being released as sound. If you were to touch the bumper on your bumper car after impact, it would feel warm. It feels warm because energy is also released as heat.

exert—to apply

Where's the Equal and Opposite Reaction?

So what happens when you stomp on the ground? Or flop on a bench? Your stomping or flopping action doesn't seem to cause a reaction from the ground or the bench. But these objects are reacting. What would happen if they weren't pushing back with an equal and opposite force? Nothing would support your foot or your bottom.

You don't see the ground or the bench react because of their inertia. The action you apply is not enough to get them to change from their states of rest.

You can feel Newton's third law when you push against your strap or bar in a wild ride. The strap is pushing back as hard as you are pushing against it. When do you feel the reaction of your strap most? It's when your action is the greatest, such as when a ride stops suddenly, and your body keeps moving.

As you push against a safety bar, the bar pushes against you.

CHAPTER 5

ALL TOGETHER NOW!

When you go hurtling down a roller coaster hill, which of Newton's laws are at work? They all are! Newton's laws are acting everywhere all the time. You can combine all the laws to explain a single event.

The force the coaster exerts on the track depends on its mass and its acceleration. Also the more massive it is and the more it's accelerating, the greater the force needed to stop it. That's Newton's second law.

When the coaster cars push on the track, the track pushes back with an equal force. This force is in the opposite direction. If this were not true, the track would buckle or the cars would fly off the track. That's Newton's third law.

And what makes the cars sail right up the next hill? That's inertia, part of Newton's first law.

The laws of motion combine for a day of fun at an amusement park!

Everywhere you go, all the time—especially at the amusement park—the laws of motion are there. Just keep looking, and you'll keep seeing them doing their work!

GLOSSARY

accelerate (ak-SEL-uh-rayt)—to change the speed of a moving object

centripetal force (sen-TRI-puh-tuhl FORS)—a force that pulls spinning objects to the center of a circle

cylindrical (suh-LIN-dri-kuhl)—having a shape with flat, circular ends and sides shaped like a tube

exert (ig-ZURT)—to apply

friction (FRIK-shuhn)—the force caused by objects rubbing together

gravity (GRAV-uh-tee)—a force that pulls objects with mass together; gravity pulls objects down toward the center of Earth

impact (im-PAKT)—a forceful contact of objects

inertia (in-UR-shuh)—the tendency of an object to stay at rest or in an existing state of motion in a straight line unless acted on by a force

mass (MAS)—the amount of material in an object

momentum (moh-MEN-tuhm)—the amount of force in a moving object determined by the object's mass and velocity

pendulum (PEN-juh-luhm)—a weight that hangs from a fixed point and swings back and forth freely using the force of gravity

physics (FIZ-iks)—the study of matter and energy, including light, heat, electricity, and motion

READ MORE

Roby, Cynthia. *Discovering STEM at the Amusement Park.* STEM in the Real World. New York: PowerKids Press, 2016.

Sohn, Emily. *A Crash Course in Forces and Motion with Max Axiom Super Scientist: 4D An Augmented Reading Science Experience.* Graphic Science 4D. North Mankato, Minn.: Capstone, 2019.

Spilsbury, Richard, and Louise Spilsbury. *Ride that Roller Coaster!: Forces at an Amusement Park.* Feel the Force. Chicago, Heinemann-Raintree, 2016.

CRITICAL THINKING QUESTIONS

1. In the high striker game, you hit a pad with a mallet to send a puck up a tower. The higher you send the puck, the higher your strength is rated. Describe how Newton's laws are at work in this game.

2. Explain how F=ma shows that it is easier to push a toy car and get it going than to push a real one.

3. Why do you think you stay in your car when a roller coaster is upside down in a loop? Use online or other resources to support your answer.

INTERNET SITES

Force and Motion
https://online.kidsdiscover.com/unit/force-and-motion?ReturnUrl=/unit/force-and-motion

How Roller Coasters Work
https://science.howstuffworks.com/engineering/structural/roller-coaster3.htm

Newton's Laws of Motion
https://www.livescience.com/46558-laws-of-motion.html

INDEX